FastTrack MUSIC INSTRUCTION

Keyboard 1

INTRODUCTION

You bought a keyboard...so now what?

Congratulations! You look great behind that keyboard. But won't your friends and family be even more impressed if you can actually play the darn thing? In just a couple of weeks, we'll have you playing some cool riffs, as well as jamming with some cool chords and songs. By the end of this book, it's on to the hits—the Beatles, Clapton, Hendrix and many more—in the *FastTrack* songbooks.

All we ask is that you observe the three Ps: **patience**, **practice** and **pace yourself**.

Don't try to bite off more than you can chew, and DON'T skip ahead. If your hands hurt, take the day off. If you get frustrated, put the book away and come back later. If you forget something, go back and learn it again. If you're having a great time, keep on playing. Most importantly, have fun.

ABOUT THE AUDIO

Glad you noticed the added bonus — audio tracks! Each music example has been recorded so you can hear how it sounds and play along when you're ready. The examples are preceded by a one-measure count-off to indicate tempo and meter. Hal Leonard's **PLAYBACK+** allows you to emphasize the keyboard part by panning right, or the accompaniment by panning left. This symbol will indicate an audio track is available for the example:

PLAYBACK+
Speed • Pitch • Balance • Loop

To access audio visit:
www.halleonard.com/mylibrary

Enter Code
2560-5653-7527-3466

ISBN: 978-0-7935-7407-0

Visit Hal Leonard Online at
www.halleonard.com

Contact Us:
Hal Leonard
7777 West Bluemound Road
Milwaukee, WI 53213
Email: info@halleonard.com

In Europe contact:
Hal Leonard Europe Limited
Distribution Centre, Newmarket Road
Bury St Edmunds, Suffolk, IP33 3YB
Email: info@halleonardeurope.com

In Australia contact:
Hal Leonard Australia Pty. Ltd.
4 Lentara Court
Cheltenham, Victoria, 3192 Australia
Email: info@halleonard.com.au

A GOOD PLACE TO START

Sitting or standing

Perhaps the most comfortable and least tiring way to learn the keyboard is to sit while playing. When sitting, make sure your keyboard isn't too high, or your arms will start hurting.

In many bands, the keyboardist stands. If you choose to stand, make sure the keyboard isn't positioned too low.

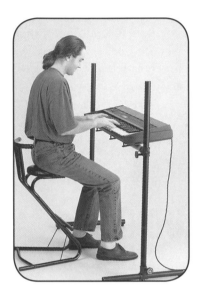
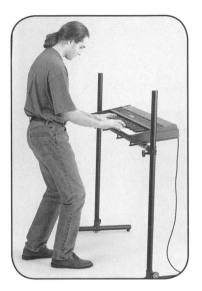

Hand position

Think of your fingers as being numbered 1 through 5—thumb is "1" and pinkie is "5."

Remember to keep your fingers arched at all times. You can play much faster and more accurately than if your fingers are flat.

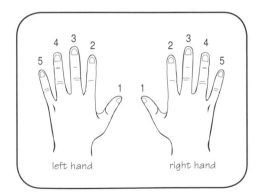

The keys to success...

Your keyboard (and anyone else's) is made up of groups of **black** and **white** keys. The black keys come in sets of two and three:

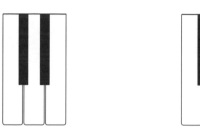

Notes on the keyboard

What note is it?

Each white key in the group has it's own note name, using the first seven letters of the alphabet:

TRACK 1

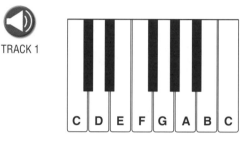

Find 'em quick!

To locate all the white keys quickly, just remember three simple rules:

 The keys are in alphabetical order: A-B-C-D-E-F-G. (If you get to "H," you've gone too far!)

 C is always before a set of two black keys:

 F is always before a set of 3 black keys:

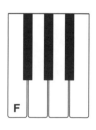

 "Are the black keys just guides?"
No. They're notes called "sharps" and "flats," which you'll learn later.

3

DOG-EAR THESE TWO PAGES

(...you'll need to review them later)

Music is a language with its own symbols, structure, rules (and exceptions to those rules). To read, write, and play music requires knowing all the symbols and rules. But let's take it one step at a time (a few now, a few later)...

Notes

Music is written with symbols called **notes.** Notes come in all shapes and sizes. A note has two essential characteristics: its **pitch** (indicated by its position) and its **rhythmic value** (indicated by the following symbols):

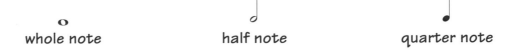

whole note　　　　　**half note**　　　　　**quarter note**

The rhythmic value lets you know how many beats the note lasts. Most commonly, a quarter note equals one beat. After that it's just like fractions:

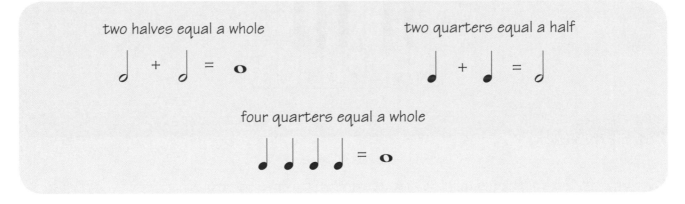

two halves equal a whole　　　　　two quarters equal a half

four quarters equal a whole

Staff

All the notes are positioned on (or nearby) a **staff**, which consists of five parallel lines and four spaces. (The plural for staff is "staves.") Each line and space represent a different pitch.

Leger Lines

Since not all notes will fit on just five lines and four spaces, **leger lines** are used to extend the staff:

Clef

A symbol called a **clef** indicates which pitches appear on a particular staff. Music uses a variety of clefs, but we're only concerned with one for now:

treble clef

A **treble clef** staff makes the lines and spaces have the following pitches:

E	G	B	D	F
Every	Good	Band	Draws	Fans

F A C E
"FACE"

An easy way to remember the line pitches is "**E**very **G**ood **B**and **D**raws **F**ans." For the spaces, spell "**face**."

Measures (or Bars)

Notes on a staff are divided into **measures** (or "bars") to help you keep track of where you are in the song.

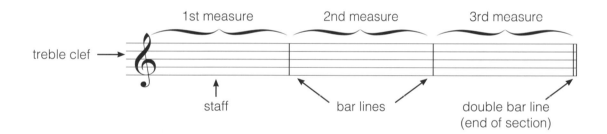

1st measure   2nd measure   3rd measure

treble clef →

staff   bar lines   double bar line
(end of section)

Time Signatures (or Meters)

A **time signature** (or "meter") indicates how many beats will appear in each measure. It contains two numbers: the top number tells you how many beats will be in each measure; the bottom number says what type of note will equal one beat.

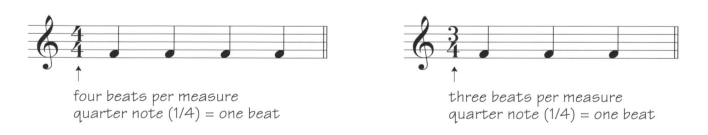

four beats per measure
quarter note (1/4) = one beat

three beats per measure
quarter note (1/4) = one beat

Relax for a while, read through it again later, and then move on.
(Trust us—as we go through the book, you'll start to understand it.)

5

LESSON 1

It's time to play something!

We're powered "on." We're relaxed. We're comfortable. And we're eager to play. Let's get down to business…

C Position: Right Hand

Find the C key that is closest to the middle of your keyboard—that's "middle C." Place Finger 1 (thumb) of your right hand on middle C and the other four fingers on the next four notes:

Let's get acquainted with these notes in a song. (Don't hesitate to turn back to pages 4 and 5 if you need to review notes and rhythm):

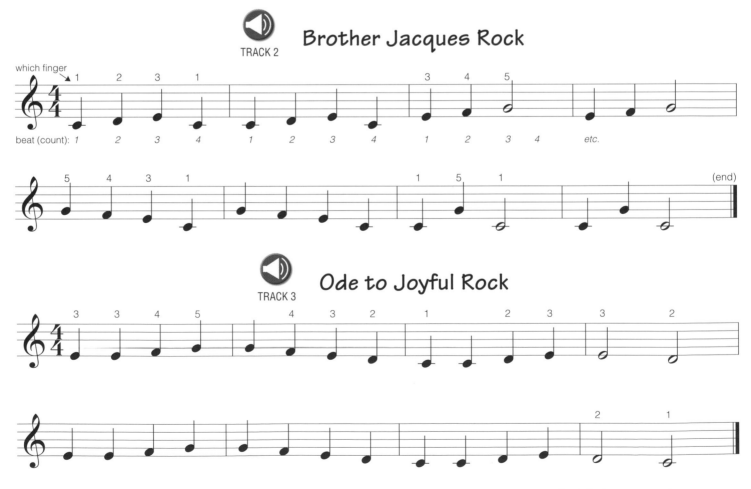

TRACK 2

Brother Jacques Rock

TRACK 3

Ode to Joyful Rock

Five notes and two songs in less than five minutes—not bad progress, huh? Practice these notes with some more well-known tunes on the next page…

Go Find the Roadie

Go find the road - ie. Go find the road - die.

Go find the road - ie, my key - board stand fell down.

Rockin' the Bells

Keep those fingers arched!

Tisket, Tasket

Repeat these tunes over and over, playing them a little bit faster each time.

SOME MORE NOTES ON MUSIC
(...pardon the pun!)

Rests

A musical **rest** is a pause. Rests are like notes in that they have their own rhythmic values, instructing you how long (or how many beats) to pause:

whole rest
(four beats)

half rest
(two beats)

quarter rest
(one beat)

Try it...

In the following 4/4 example, you will play G, G, pause, G, pause, pause, pause, pause, G, G, pause, pause, G, pause, pause, G:

Take a Load Off
TRACK 7

count out loud: 1   2 (3) 4   (1 2 3 4) 1 2 (3 4) 1 (2 3) 4

IMPORTANT: A rest does not mean put your hands down or rest your fingers! During a rest, you should read ahead and ready your fingers for the next set of notes.

Rock, Roll, Rest
TRACK 8

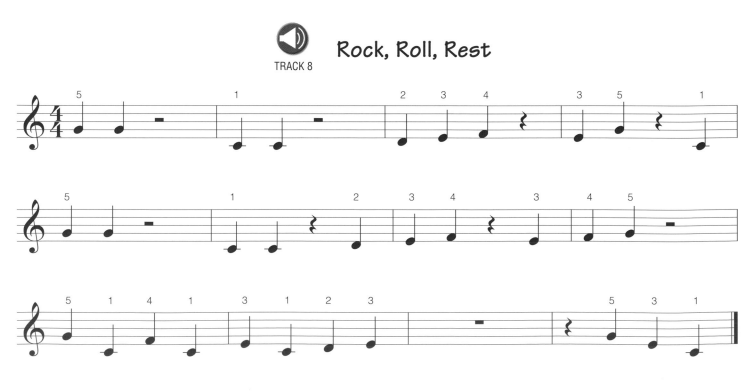

Pickups

Instead of starting a song with rests, a **pickup measure** can be used. A pickup measure simply deletes the rests. So, if a pickup has only one beat, you count "1, 2, 3" and start playing on beat 4:

Try these songs with pickup measures:

When the Saints Go Marching In
TRACK 9

NOTE: The last measure contains the missing beats from the pickup measure.

Pickup and Shuffle
TRACK 10

☞ Great! Practice the songs from Lesson 1 again.
When you're ready, move on to Lesson 2.

LESSON 2

Not too much of a stretch...

Welcome back! Now you know five notes, some songs, and how to rest. But there are only so many songs you can play with C, D, E, F, and G. Let's learn two more notes...

Thumb and pinkie notes: B and A

With your hand in C Position, move Finger 1 (thumb) one key lower to B. Now try moving Finger 5 (pinkie) one key higher to A.

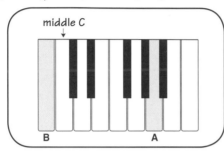

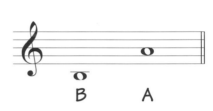

Try out these two new notes with the following two songs...

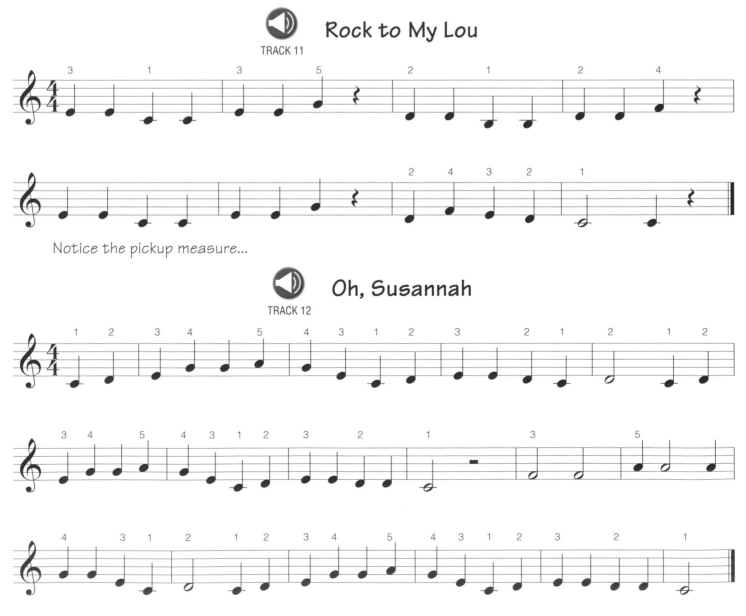

Rock to My Lou

TRACK 11

Notice the pickup measure...

Oh, Susannah

TRACK 12

Always practice slowly at first. Speed up the **tempo** only as you become more confident with the notes.

Danny Boy

TRACK 13

REMINDER: The next song is in 3/4 meter. That is, it has three beats (quarter notes) per measure. (For a quick review of meters, flip back to page 5.)

Chiapanecas

TRACK 14

Watch the music, not your fingers!
(Your brain has enough going on—don't try to memorize the tunes, too!)

YOU GOT RHYTHM

Ties

A **tie** connects two notes and tells you to hold the first note through to the end of the tied note:

count: 1 2 3 4 1 2 3 4 1 2 3 4 1 2 3 (4)
hold hold hold

Simple! Remember to always count out loud until you begin to think and feel the beat.

Kum-bah-yah

TRACK 15

Kum - bah - yah my Lord, _____ Kum - bah - yah, _____

_____ Kum - bah - yah my Lord, _____ Kum - bah - yah, _____

_____ Kum - bah - yah my Lord, _____ Kum - bah - yah, _____

_____ oh, Lord _____ Kum - bah - yah. _____

Dots

Another way to extend the value of a note is to use a **dot**. A dot extends the note by one-half of its value. Most common is the **dotted half** note:

half note + dot = dotted half note
(two beats) (one beat) (three beats)

You will encounter dotted half notes in many songs, especially those that use 3/4 meter.

count: 1 2 3 1 2 3 1 2 3 1 2 3

Put it to use!

Now try some songs with ties and dots...

TRACK 16   Fit to Be Tied

My key - board has black keys and white keys. My key - board has lots of cool sounds.

I'm learn - ing to play it, be pa - tient.

And soon I'll be rock - ing this town.

My Keyboard

TRACK 17

This is a good time to take a break.
Then come back, review the songs, and move on to Lesson 3.

LESSON 3
Two hands are better than one...

Unbelievable—seven notes, rests, ties, dots and some songs! "But shouldn't both hands be playing?" You're way ahead of us...

C Position: Left Hand

Find the next C below middle C and place finger 5 of your left hand on this key. The next four fingers lay on the next four notes up, as shown:

NOTE: Just like the right hand, extend your thumb and pinkie (Fingers 1 and 5) to play A and B in the left hand.

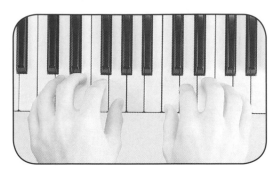

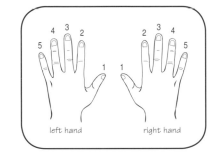

One at a time...

The left hand can provide **harmony** by playing and holding notes while the right hand plays the melody. In the following songs, the names of the notes to be played (and held) by the left hand are shown above the staff:

Harmony Warm-Up

TRACK 18

Now add harmony to some well known tunes...

Aura Lee

TRACK 19

☞ **Repeat signs** have two dots before or after an end barline (‖: :‖). They simply tell you to repeat everything in between. Only one repeat sign at the end tells you to repeat from the beginning.

Marianne

TRACK 20

The next song has a **1st** and **2nd ending** (indicated by brackets and the numbers "1" and "2"). Play the song once to the repeat sign (1st ending), then repeat from measure 2. The second time through, skip the 1st ending and play the 2nd (last) ending...

Michael, Rock the Crowd Ashore

TRACK 21

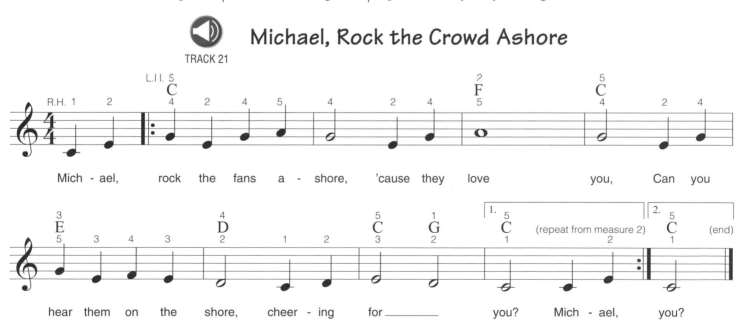

HELPFUL HINT: Let your eyes read ahead of the note that you're actually playing. That way, you will know what's coming and ready your fingers early.

LESSON 4
Fear of flying solo...

The single-note harmony you've been playing sounds fine, but how 'bout making a fuller sound? It's time to learn some **chords**.

What is a chord?

A chord consists of three or more notes played simultaneously. Listen to some examples of chords on the audio:

TRACK 22   C   G   F   Am   Em

Knowing chords is essential because:

1 Chords provide harmony for the melody that you (or another band member) are playing.

2 If you don't feel like playing a solo, simply play the chords of a song while you sing the melody.

3 Major chords...

Believe it or not, with the seven notes you already know, you can play lots of chords.

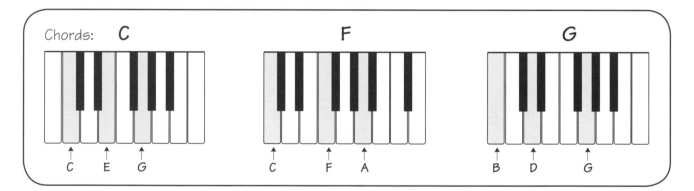

2-FOR-1 SPECIAL: You can play these chords with either hand in C Position. (Just use any "C" as a guide and build the correct chords from there.)

Put 'em to work...

Choose a hand and practice your new chords:

TRACK 23   C – F – C – G   C – F – G – C   F – G – C

Now switch hands and repeat the exercise. Then try it with both hands at the same time!

No longer single...

From now on, instead of single-note harmony, the letters above the staff are **chord symbols**, indicating which chords to play in the left hand.

Using these chord symbols, play only the chords of the next song, while you sing the melody...

Twinkle, Twinkle, Little (Rock) Star

TRACK 24

Now repeat the song, playing the melody with the right hand and the chords with the left.

Chord Boogie

TRACK 25

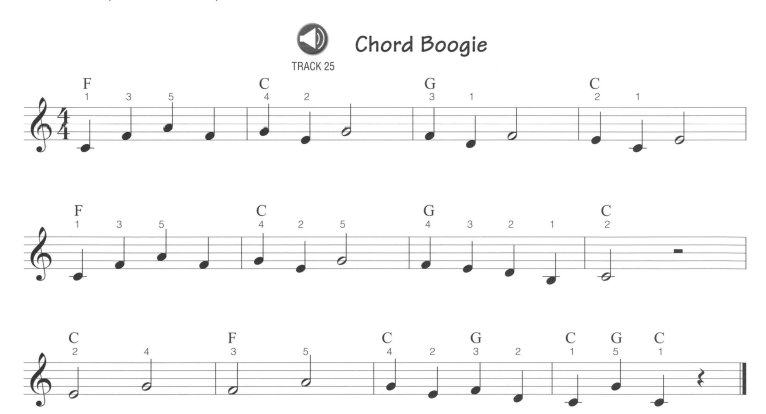

LESSON 5
It's the minor things that count...

Major chords weren't that tough, huh? How about three **minor** chords?

Chords: Em, Am, and Dm

A **chord suffix** tells you what type of chord to play. (Major chords have no suffix, only the letter name.) Minor chords use the suffix "m" after the letter name.

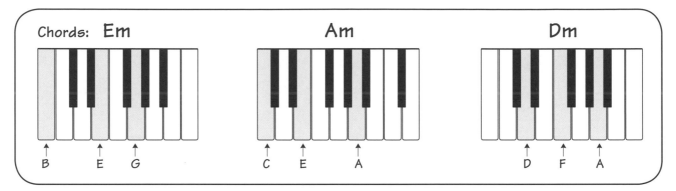

Put 'em to work...

Play your new chords, first in the right hand, then left, then both:

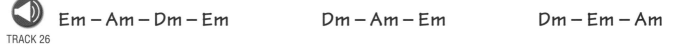

TRACK 26   Em – Am – Dm – Em   Dm – Am – Em   Dm – Em – Am

Now mix the minor chords with your major chords:

TRACK 27   C – F – Dm   Am – Em – G   Am – F – Dm – Em – C

A minor question...

As you can hear (and see), a major chord is no bigger (or any more important) than a minor one, it's just a name. So what's the difference between them? Play and listen to them again. QUICK AND EASY: Major chords sound "happy" and minor chords sound "sad."

🔊 Minor Bird Blues
TRACK 28

Music Makes Me Happy

TRACK 29

In some music arrangements, you will see **slash notation**. This simply tells you to play the chord once for every time you see a " / " symbol.

Rockin' Chords #1

TRACK 30

Rockin' Chords #2

TRACK 31

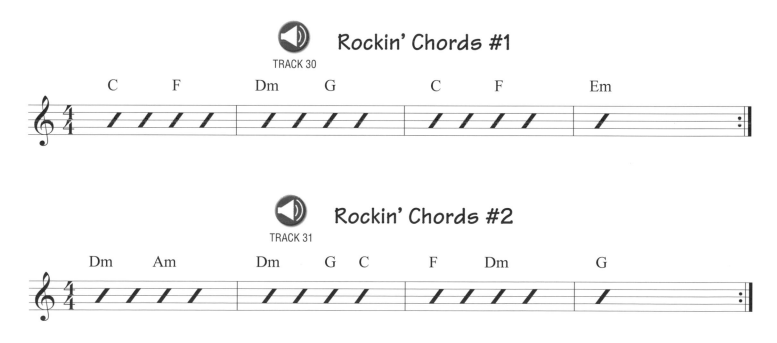

Play the two "Rockin' Chords" again and slam down both hands at once!

YOU STILL GOT RHYTHM

Can you spare a quarter? How 'bout an eighth?

An **eighth note** has a flag on it:

Two eighth notes equal one quarter note (or one beat.) To make it easier on the eyes, eighth notes are connected with a **beam**:

To count eighth notes, divide the beat into two and use "and" between the beats:

Practice this by first counting out loud while tapping your foot on the beat, then play the notes while counting and tapping:

What about the rest?

Eighth rests are the same, but you...pause. Count, tap, play, and pause with the following:

Now try a song that uses eighth notes. (Keep that foot going!)

Rockin' Riff

TRACK 32

20

LESSON 6
Gee, we like this one!

We need some higher notes, but let's not stretch your hands too far. Simply change positions...

G Position

Put Finger 1 on the G above "middle C" and lay the other four fingers on A, B, C and D.

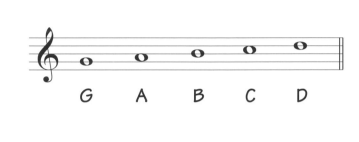

G   A   B   C   D

☞ CHANGING POSITIONS: To change from C to G position, cross finger 1 (thumb) under at an appropriate place in the music.

In this tune, as finger 4 plays F, cross your thumb under to play G. Continue playing the higher notes with your hand now in the G Position:

C to G
TRACK 33

To return to C Position, cross finger 3 over to play the E and finish the song in C Position:

Rock and Roll Your Boat
TRACK 34

21

Let's stretch again...

In G Position, Finger 1 moves down to F; Finger 5 moves up to E.

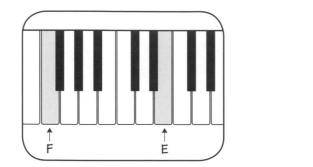

Try out your new notes with this tune:

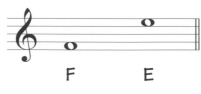

F – E Workout

TRACK 35

☞ NEW FINGERING: When changing positions, it's sometimes necessary to move the entire hand (rather than crossing fingers). In the next song, move your hand between positions where indicated.

Bach Rock

TRACK 36

Play it again. Make sure you are using the correct fingering in the right hand.

YOU LOOK SHARP!

Music is made up of **half steps** and **whole steps**. From one key to the next closest key (whether white or black) is a half step.

One half step higher is called a **sharp** and looks like a tic-tac-toe board: ♯

One half-step lower is called a **flat** and looks like a lower-case b: ♭

IMPORTANT: A sharp or flat symbol is only used once on the same note in a measure. That is, if one A has a flat, then all A's in that measure are A-flat.

Hava Nagilah
TRACK 37

NOTE: To play a black key, use the same finger that would play the nearest white key. For example, in C Position, use Finger 3 for E-flat, Finger 4 for F-sharp, and so on...

Bluesy Riff
TRACK 38

LESSON 7
More for your money...

More chords

With your new knowledge of sharps and flats, we can play some more cool chords...

REMINDER: A flat is the next key to the left, a sharp is the next key to the right.

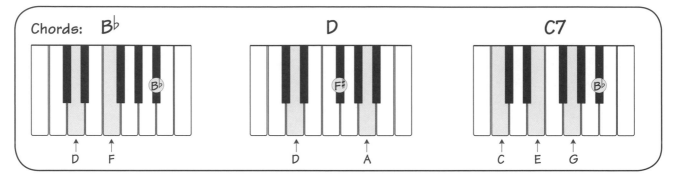

Just like before, play your new chords (along with the old ones), first in the right hand, then left, then both:

TRACK 39

G – C – D   F – B♭ – C7   G – D – Em   F – C – C7

"C7? But it has four notes!"

Correct. Notice a difference between the C and C7 chords? The suffix "7" indicates that the basic C chord has a little addition (sure, a fourth note!): a 7th-chord adds a bit of musical "tension" to make the ear want musical "relief."

Listen again to the chords above. Your ear wants more after the 7th-chord? Then here's more music...

Good Night, My Fans

TRACK 40

*Change to the thumb while holding the note.

Red River Rockin'

TRACK 41

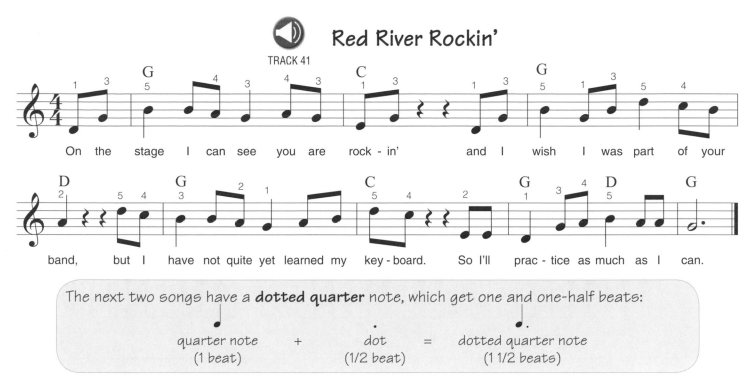

On the stage I can see you are rock-in' and I wish I was part of your band, but I have not quite yet learned my key-board. So I'll prac-tice as much as I can.

The next two songs have a **dotted quarter** note, which get one and one-half beats:

quarter note + dot = dotted quarter note
(1 beat)   (1/2 beat)   (1 1/2 beats)

Listen to the next two songs on the audio while you clap the beat. Can you feel the rhythm of the dotted quarter? Try playing it.

Swingin' That Old Chariot

TRACK 42

Worried Man Blues

TRACK 43

It takes a wor-ried man to sing a wor-ried song. It takes a wor-ried man to sing a wor-ried song. It takes a wor-ried man to sing a wor-ried song. I'm wor-ried now, but I won't be wor-ried long.

7th-chords

To build a 7th-chord, simply play a major or minor chord and add a fourth note that is one **whole step** lower than the note that names the chord. (Remember half steps from page 23? From one key to the next closest key is a half step, and two half steps equal one whole step. Therefore, to move one whole step, you just skip one key in between.)

Try some...

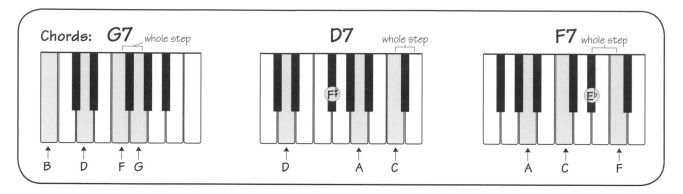

How about playing B♭7?

Here's a well-known tune with 7th-chords. Play it first as written. Then try substituting all 7th-chords. Which sound do you like better?

Play it again, but try **rolling** the chords. That is, don't strike them all at once. Start with the lowest note and quickly roll into the chord. Try rolling from top to bottom, too...

Progress is good...

In most music, chords follow a certain pattern of switching called **chord progressions**. Notice how the chords "progress" in this well-known tune:

Little Rock Band

TRACK 45

The next example uses a common two-measure chord progression similar to many rock songs, including "Louie, Louie" and "Wild Thing."

Three-Chord Cliché

TRACK 46

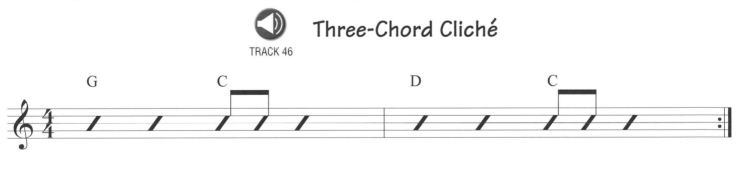

Here's another rockin' chord progression.

Chord Jam

TRACK 47

LESSON 8
Reaching higher

So far, Fingers 1 and 5 have only stretched one key higher or lower. Well, crack those knuckles and get ready...

High F

In G Position, extend Finger 5 up to F:

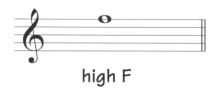

high F

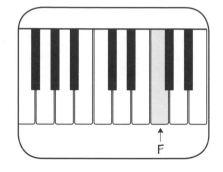

Congratulations! You've learned all the lines and spaces of the treble clef staff. Let's try out your new note:

Fast-Paced Blues
TRACK 48

SHORT CUT: Instead of writing a symbol by every sharp or flat in a song, a **key signature** is used. A key signature with a flat on the B-line tells you to play all Bs as B-flat...

Rockin' on Old Smoky
TRACK 49

If you're going to play up high for a while, you might as well change positions instead of stretching. (Plus, you can learn a few more notes!) Move your hand up and put your thumb on "high F" and the other four fingers on high G, A, B, and C:

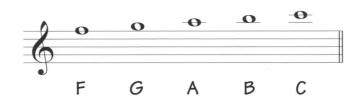

F   G   A   B   C

NEW RULE: A **natural sign** (♮) cancels a sharp or flat on a note, returning the note to its "natural" pitch (or white key), but only for that measure.

Star-Spangled Banner

TRACK 50

Why bother stretching?

The stretch you made to "high F" is a 7th **interval**. An interval is the distance between two notes. Intervals come in all shapes and sizes and help us build chords and harmony. Use the staff lines and spaces to help you recognize intervals by sight:

3rds
one line (or space) apart

4ths
one line and one space apart

5ths
two lines (or spaces) apart

Try this riff with 3rds, 4ths and 5ths...

Little Interval Groove

TRACK 51

The bigger the interval, the farther apart the notes are...

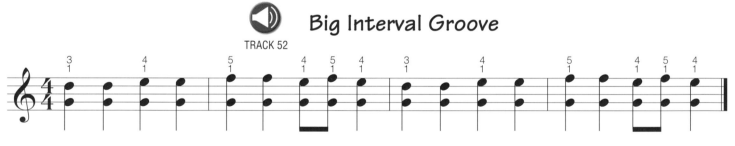

6ths

7ths

Now a riff with 5ths, 6ths and 7ths...

Big Interval Groove

TRACK 52

The right hand can add intervals to the melody for a fuller sound...

Interval Blues

TRACK 53

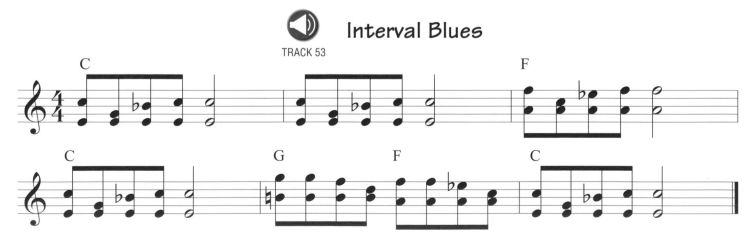

Now for the ultimate stretch...

LESSON 9
From C to shining C...

With your right hand in C position, extend finger 5 up to the next C:

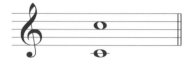

That interval is called an **octave**. An octave simply means eight notes apart. From any note on the keyboard to the note above (or below) **with the same letter name** is an octave.

You can use a 5th interval to help you reach an octave:

Also Sprach Rock
TRACK 54

Now try some octave intervals. Practice slowly...

Giant Leaps
TRACK 55

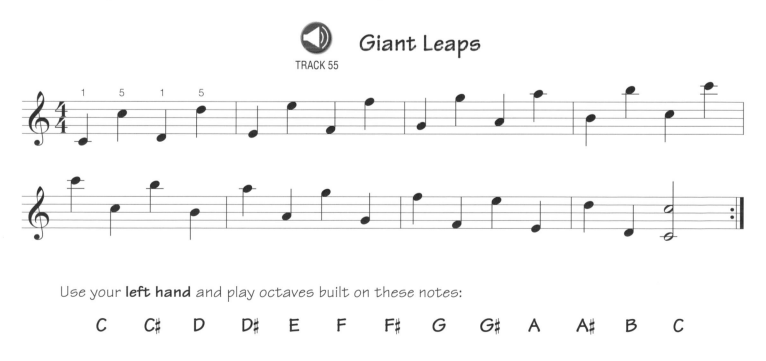

Use your **left hand** and play octaves built on these notes:

C   C♯   D   D♯   E   F   F♯   G   G♯   A   A♯   B   C

Turn up the bass!

You can use your new left-hand octaves to accompany chords in the right hand. For example, play a G chord in the right hand while playing a G octave in the left.

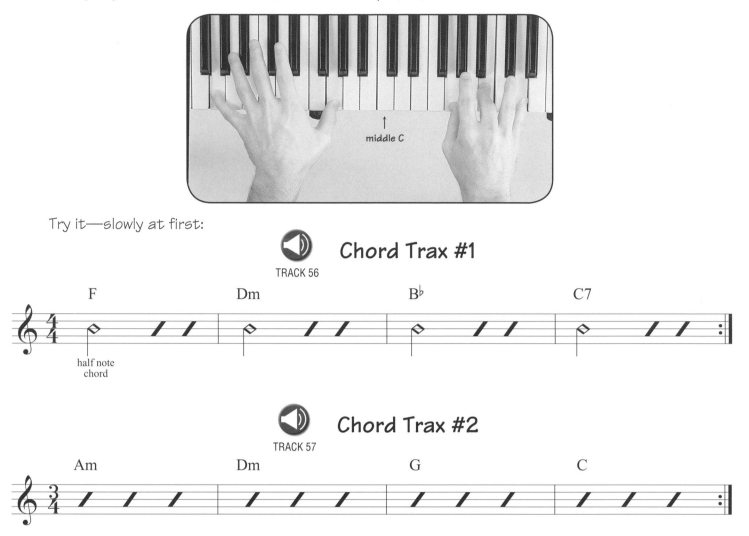

Try it—slowly at first:

Chord Trax #1
TRACK 56

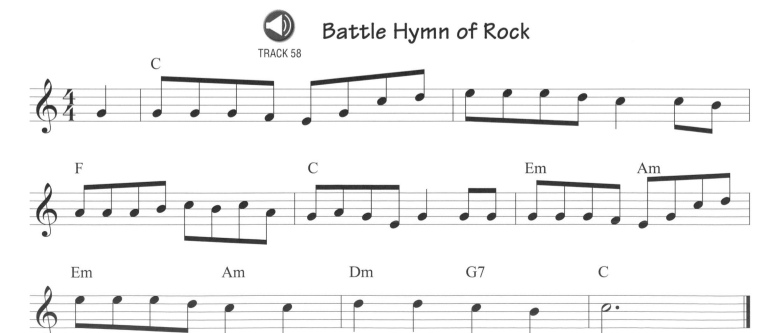

Chord Trax #2
TRACK 57

Play this tune with your new "bass-octave" accompaniment style. Play chords with the right hand, octaves with the left and sing the well-known melody…

Battle Hymn of Rock
TRACK 58

Of course, octave intervals are also found in melodies of songs…

Run, Don't Walk

TRACK 59

WARNING: Notice the new key signature. It places a sharp on the F-line. Unless you see a natural sign (♮), play all Fs as F-sharp.

Take Me Onto the Stage, Please

TRACK 60

Take me on - to the stage, please, out in front of the crowd. _____ I want to play all these songs for them. I'll be rock - in' so turn it up loud. All I want to do is play mu - sic, rock, jazz, or blues, I don't care. _____ So come on, please, show me the way to the stage out there!

Give your hands a rest, review these songs again later, and then we'll discuss a new playing style…

YOU GOT STYLE!

Sliding and gliding...

A nice effect in keyboard music is a **glissando** (or "gliss"). It means to slide your finger from one note to another, dragging it across the other keys in between.

A

Turn your hand over and drag Finger 2 up across the keys.

B

Raise your fingers and drag your thumbnail down across the keys.

Glissandos are most commonly used between notes that are an octave apart but you can gliss any size interval. Try these...

TRACK 61

Put those slides to the test with a tune...

Gliss This!

TRACK 62

If it ain't broke, break it!

A chord can be played one note at a time, back and forth. Play a C chord. Then play its notes one at a time:

That's a **broken chord**. You can make any chord into a broken chord (just use the chord symbols as a guide):

Break It in Threes

TRACK 63

In 4/4 meter, play the chord notes up and then back down:

Break It in Fours

TRACK 64

Break it a little faster by using eighth notes:

Faster Broken Chords

TRACK 65

Options are nice...

Play broken chords in the left hand to make a great-sounding accompaniment. Simply put your hand in position for the chord and play each note of the chord up and down. Try breaking these chords:

C   F   G   B♭   Em   Am   Dm

Don't forget to use this option as you continue to play songs in the book...

LESSON 10
Scales

You know all the lines and spaces on the staff, as well as some leger lines on top and bottom. Let's play all the white keys and travel up two octaves. (Make sure you use the correct fingering!)

C to C to C

TRACK 66

Do you realize what you just played? That was your first musical **scale**—C Major. And a two-octave scale at that!

What's a musical scale?

Scales are arrangements of notes in specific patterns of half-steps and whole-steps. Most scales have eight notes with the top and bottom notes being an octave apart. The one you just played started on C and used a **major pattern**, thus it was the C Major scale.

Here are two more (single octave) major scales (notice the key signatures!)...

G Major Scale

TRACK 67

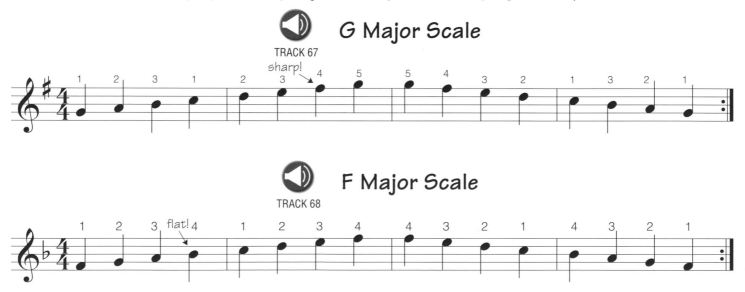

F Major Scale

TRACK 68

Major vs. minor...

Just like with chords, major scales are no more important than minor scales. The difference between the two is the specific pattern of half-steps and whole-steps used to form the scale. Play the major scales again.

Scale patterns

The pattern for a **major scale** is:

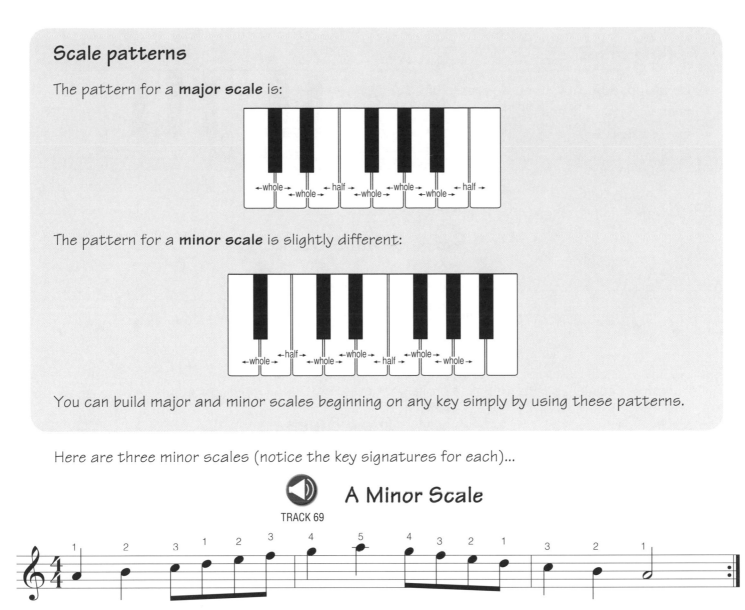

The pattern for a **minor scale** is slightly different:

You can build major and minor scales beginning on any key simply by using these patterns.

Here are three minor scales (notice the key signatures for each)...

A Minor Scale
TRACK 69

E Minor Scale
TRACK 70

D Minor Scale
TRACK 71

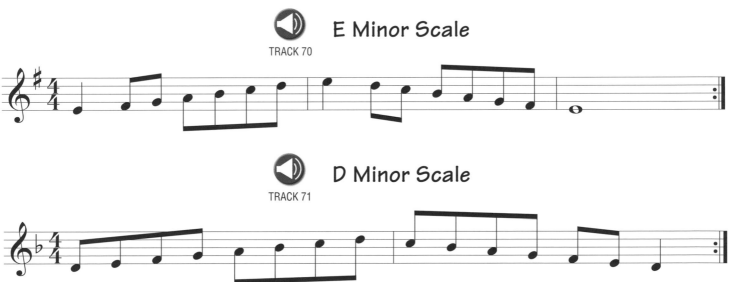

Why practice scales?

1. Knowing scales helps you build intervals and chords to accompany your melody.

2. Practicing scales helps to limber up the fingers.

Feeling blue?

The **blues scale** is closely related to the minor scale, but it has its own pattern:

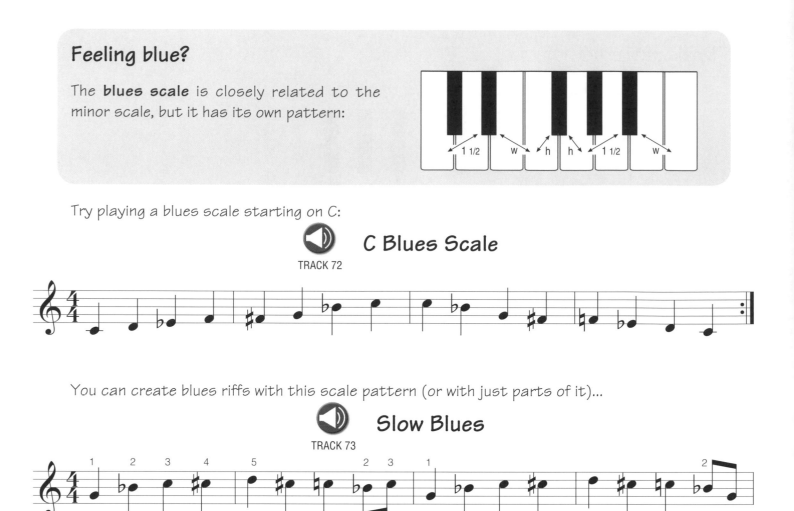

Try playing a blues scale starting on C:

C Blues Scale

TRACK 72

You can create blues riffs with this scale pattern (or with just parts of it)...

Slow Blues

TRACK 73

A bit faster now with eighth notes...

Fast Blues

TRACK 74

☞ **U**se this scale to create blues scales and riffs for other keys.

LESSON 11
Some final notes...

Y‍ou learned two leger lines on top of the staff. Let's not neglect the bottom...

New Notes: Low A and G

Return to C Position and extend your thumb down one and two keys past B.

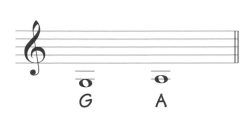

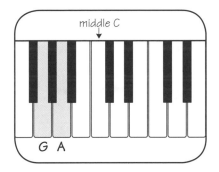

OPTIONS: Extend your thumb if you need to play these low notes only briefly. However, if the melody is down low for a while, simply shift your right hand down to a **low G Position**.

Let's try out your new notes...

Scarborough Fair

TRACK 75

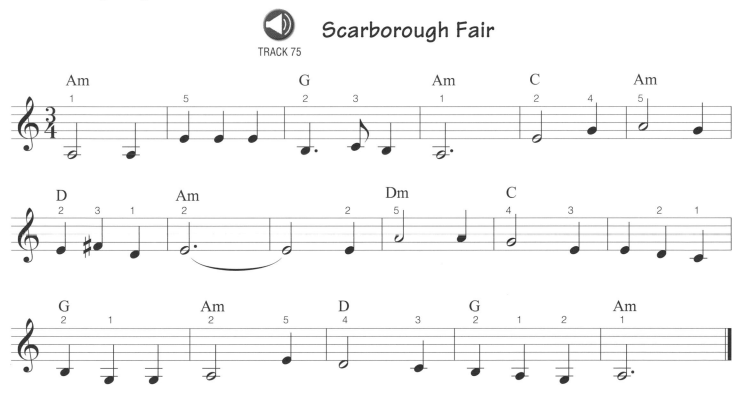

Notice that you've already played these two notes in some left hand chords. If you need to play a note that is shared by the left hand, simply lift your left hand finger off the note and return it when the right hand gets out of the way.

FINGERING TIP: Sometimes you'll find it much quicker and smoother
to cross Finger 3 over your thumb to play the lower notes B, A, and G.

Yankee Doodle Rock

TRACK 76

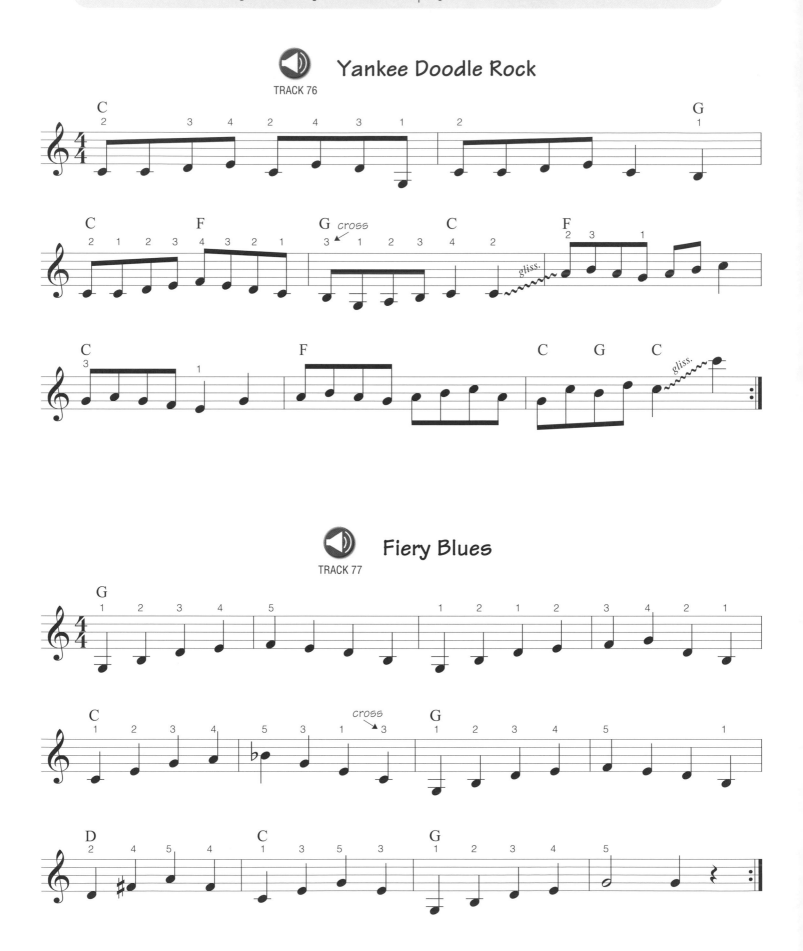

Fiery Blues

TRACK 77

LESSON 12
Everything and the kitchen sync...

Finally, let us tell you about one of the most essential (and fun) rhythmic concepts in music...

Syncopation

Syncopation is simply playing notes "off the beat." It makes the music sound less predictable. Listen to a non-syncopated example:

Not Quite

TRACK 78

Now, listen to the same example **with** syncopation:

Just Right

TRACK 79

You can still feel the beat, but it certainly has a hipper groove to it.

Your turn!

Try playing these songs with syncopation. Stress the notes that have an accent mark "**>**" below them (most of which will not be on the downbeat)…

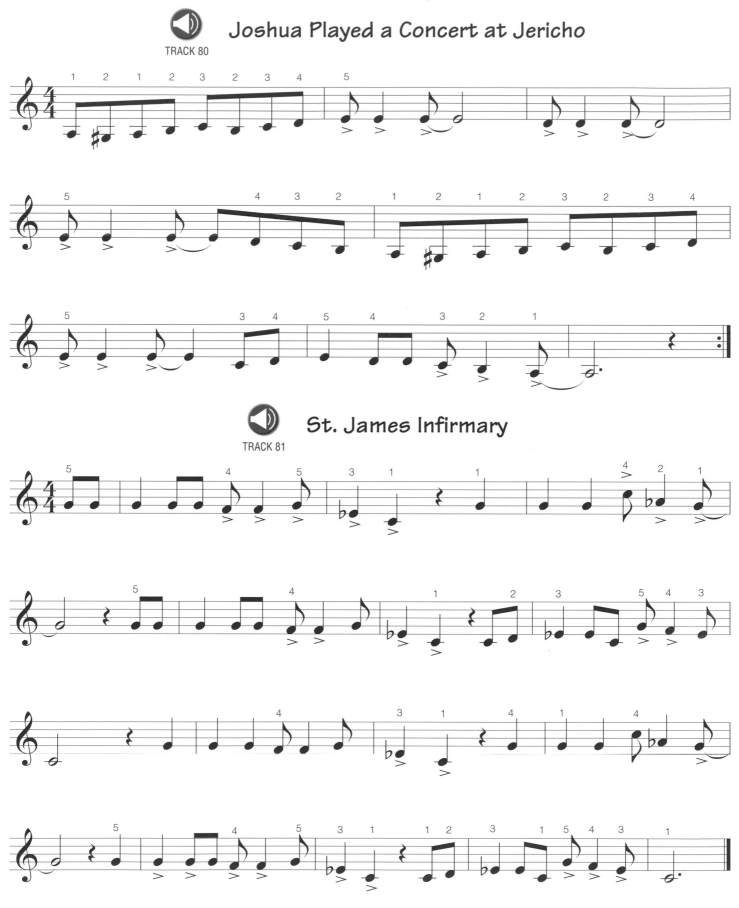

Joshua Played a Concert at Jericho
TRACK 80

St. James Infirmary
TRACK 81

Terrific! Here are some more syncopations…

You've Got a Keyboard in Your Hands

TRACK 82

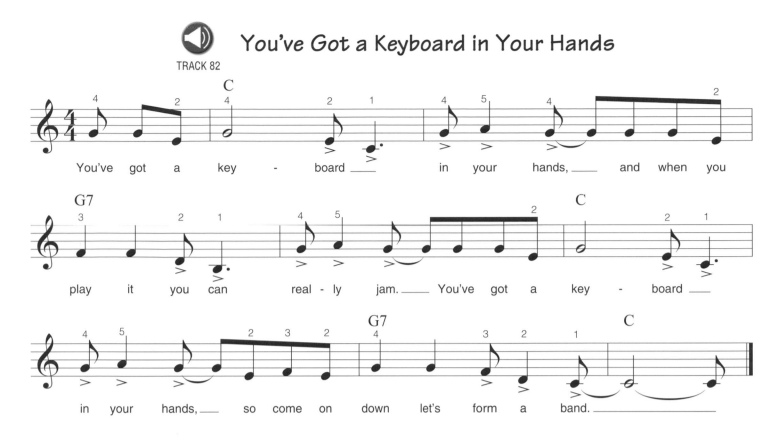

You've got a key - board _____ in your hands, _____ and when you play it you can real - ly jam. _____ You've got a key - board _____ in your hands, _____ so come on down let's form a band. _____

Allow your left hand to stress chords "off the beat," too...

Chord Trax #3

TRACK 83

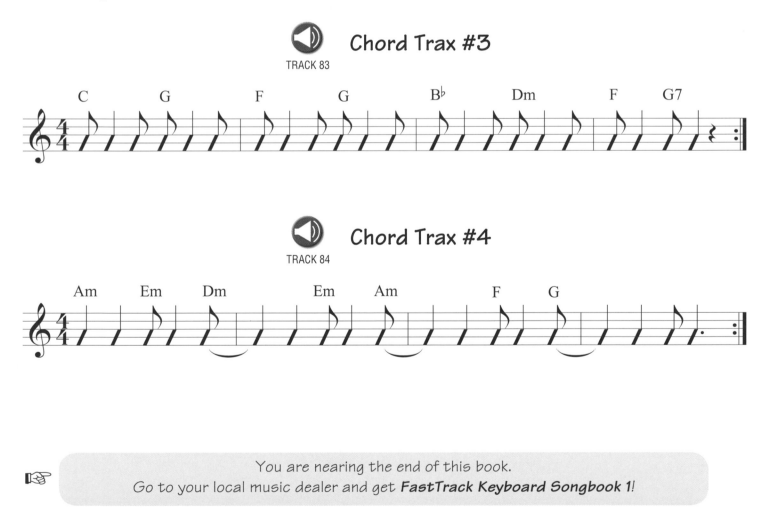

Allow your left hand to stress chords "off the beat," too...

Chord Trax #4

TRACK 84

You are nearing the end of this book.
Go to your local music dealer and get **FastTrack Keyboard Songbook 1!**

LESSON 13
Time to charge admission...

This isn't really a Lesson...it's a jam session!

All the *FastTrack* books (guitar, keyboard, bass, and drums) have the same last section. This way, you can either play by yourself along with the audio or form a band with your friends.

So, whether the band's on the audio tracks or in your garage, let the show begin...

TRACK 85
full
band

TRACK 86
minus
keyboard

Exit for Freedom

Unplugged Ballad

A **Intro**
Moderately Slow

B **Verse**

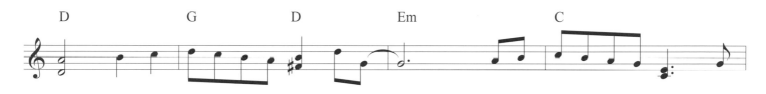

C **Chorus**

D **Bridge**

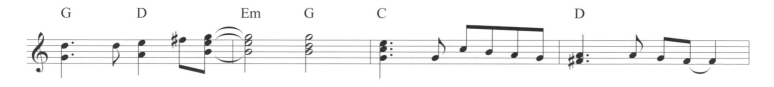

E **Outro**

45

Billy B. Badd

WAIT! DON'T GO YET!

Even though we hope (and expect) that you will review this entire book again and again, we thought you might like a "cheat sheet," referencing all the chords you learned.

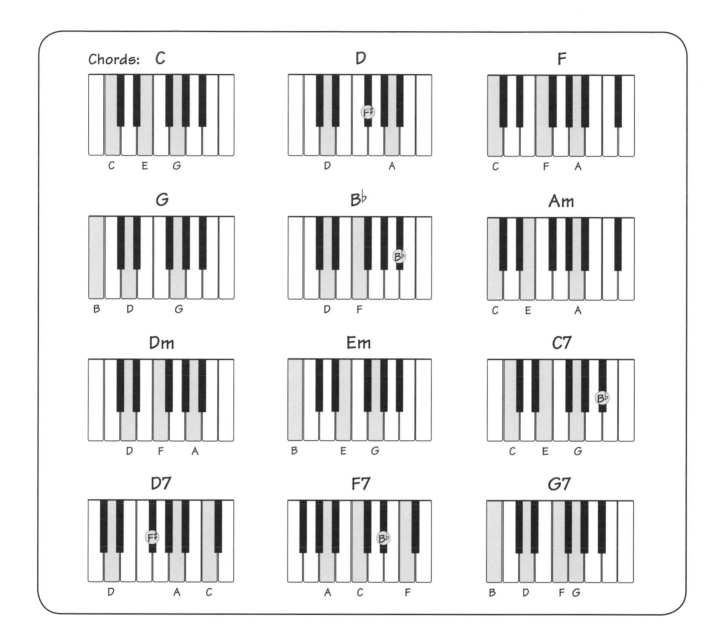

"What do I do now?"

Finally, we want to suggest a few things to help you continue to master the keyboard:

 Repetition is the best way to learn. Review the exercises in this book again and again until all the notes and chords are easily playable without even thinking about them.

 Buy *FastTrack Keyboard: Chords and Scales,* an excellent reference book with basic chord theory, scales, modes, and common chord progressions.

 Enjoy what you do. Whether it's practicing, jamming, performing, or even dusting your keyboard, do it with a smile on your face. Life's too short.

See you next time...

SONG INDEX